THE

INDEX FUNDS LAUNCHPAD

An essential handbook to index funds fundamentals and how to start the first profitable investment

Michael C. Graham

Table of Contents

Introduction

Congratulations on buying *The Index Funds Launchpad: An essential handbook to index funds fundamentals and how to start the first profitable investment* and thank you for doing so. It is normal for you to have jitters, worrying about how things will turn out especially when it comes to placing your trust and precious possessions like your life savings in the hands of other people, with the hope that beating the odds, the investment will grow.

The investment world is such a tumultuous one, filled with stocks, bonds, and other securities each performing differently, as well as the brutal forces of demand and supply and navigating which make it seem impossible. However, it is in this mire that people get massive profits and good returns on their investment, and you too should get a portion of it if you take the right investment vehicle.

For persons who are risk-averse, do not know much about the investment market, and do not desire active engagement yet want the returns of investing, Index Funds Investment is for you. Investing in this way involves the purchase of an index fund that will consequently follow the performance of an underlying index. An index is similar to pack whose contents are stocks, bonds, or both drawn from various companies, depending on the rules and the selection criteria for each index. You will need a little more detail to understand these facts fully so that you can begin your investment journey immediately.

To that end, the following chapters will unearth concepts surrounding Index Funds, using a friendly language that introduces you to the world of investing. You will find information explaining index funds and a clear explanation to differentiate index funds, ETFs, and actively-managed funds. You will also see a comprehensive list of advantages meant to unearth to you the incredible benefits you can expect when you purchase index funds and an accompanying list of things to be wary about when investing. You will also find suggestions of the best index funds to buy. These details, among others, will get you on your feet, enable you to make sound investment decisions, and equip you to teach others about the same.

There are plenty of books on this subject on the market, so thanks again for choosing this one! Every effort was made to ensure it is full of as much useful information as possible. Last but not least, get your bonus Top 10 index funds to kickstart your first investment by the end of this book. Please enjoy!

Chapter 1: Explaining the Index Fund

Every financial adviser you will meet gushes over the need to invest in mutual funds such as index funds, and they have a point. Index funds are popular for many reasons—they are a low cost, diversified, easy and hands-off way to invest in the stock market.

All the same, many of us have heard the phrase "index funds" or read a piece of writing that mentioned it, but it floated away without our understanding of what it actually meant. Well, this chapter dives into the mire of financial facts and knowledge to enlighten you on this incredible form of investment to get you making the elusive passive income you have always desired. You could even become an expert and teach others.

Like most people, it is likely that you have never heard of John Bogle. He came up with the index funds concept and is also the Vanguard Group founder. The investment world does not give him as much recognition and credit as he deserves, especially now that he went on forced retirement and left his company under management. However, this man was a fierce voice in the mutual funds' sphere. He has long talked about the high fees that companies charge and their lack of accountability to the shareholders, excessive taxation, and other constraints within the fund.

Bogle is not only vocal about the lack of or inadequate professionalism in the industry but also has some advice for investors concerning about picking the right index funds to invest in. Bogle believes that it is impossible to know how to choose the right individual stocks as well as to buy each just at the right time. In fact, if each person tries to beat and outsmart each other in the market, then the society will be trying to trick itself, which is unwise. Instead, Bogle came up with the index fund as a way of getting rid of all investment constraints. Hc believed that index funds would take out all the risks brought by individual stocks, the market, and the management, leaving the investors to juggle stock market risks.

The Index Funds

Index fund by definition is an exchange-traded fund or a mutual fund that is designed in a way that matches the returns the investors would acquire from the ownership of all securities that are in a stock market index like the Standard & Poor's 500 (S & P 500) and the FTSE 100 Index. The performance of the securities themselves in the stock market reflects the performance of the index funds.

The index fund follows a number of pre-determined rules to ensure that it keeps track of the specified underlying investments. One of the rules is that an index should track dominant indexes such as the S & P 500, the Dow Jones Industrial Average, or the FTSE 100. There are also other rules that govern areas related to tracking error minimization, tax management, and the kind of trading strategies that traders take up in their quest to increase their profits and reduce the costs of trading. Some index funds even have CSR rules based on social and sustainability concerns.

When you invest in index funds, just as the name suggests, you purchase an index. The cost of buying the index is equal to the value of the stocks therein. Each index contains a varied selection of stocks packaged together, taking out the need to purchase individual stocks. Because of this, an index performs in tandem with the stocks it is tracking, except for the small deficit called a tracking error.

Index funds track the performance of an index passively unlike other actively-managed funds. At all points, index funds do not outperform the market; they merely follow in the steps of the performance of the index. In addition, since their portfolios are not managed actively, in the buy and sell fashion meant to generate profit, it is cheaper to maintain and manage them compared to those that are actively managed.

Sometimes, some schemes are not able to match the performance of the index, which means that the index funds are not of equal value to the index. This is the tracking error mentioned earlier, and it is vital for an investor to keep a close eye on this figure when making index fund investment decisions. The tracking error shows the extent of deviation of the index fund's returns from the index it is tracking. A low tracking error indicates good performance and vice versa.

Each index fund has unique rules for all the stocks included in it. These rules are called the rules of construction, and they set the standards for the companies that wish to be included in that particular index. For example, S & P 500 Index Fund, which is the most common index fund in the U.S., follows the rules set by the S & P Dow Jones Indices to govern the S & P Index. The FTSE 100 index tracks large company stocks from 100 of the largest companies traded in the London Stock Exchange. An equity index fund would include stocks that share characteristics like profitability, value, size, and the companies' geographical locations. It may also only include companies from the United Kingdom, the United States, the emerging markets, Non-US, or from companies in the Frontier Market.

Index funds drawn from the same geographical location may be divided further to include the indexes of companies based on factors like the companies being small, medium-sized, large, large value, small value, real estate, investment capital, small growth, large growth, fixed income or gross profitability, among other like factors. Company stock is purchased and placed in the specified index fund after meeting the parameters or rules. Those that move out of the parameters are sold. The primary advantage of an index fund is that an investor does not need to take much time to manage the index or spend time analyzing different stocks and their portfolios. In fact, many investors lack the knowledge, skills, and experience needed to make decisions like this.

Index Funds vs Actively-Managed Funds

From your reading so far, you have learned that Index Funds are the preferred mutual fund option because they are easier to select and cheaper to manage. You have also learned that they fetch higher returns than actively-managed funds because you pay less in taxes and the fees you have to pay are lesser because index funds are not traded all the time.

Normally, trading companies will charge a fee for every sale or purchase, and since index funds are long-term investments, you are in the market less often. Actively managed funds, on the other hand, are traded all the time, which increases the fees and taxes charged, making them an expensive option. However, it is important to note that each has its special advantage and taking note of each method's selling points will help you make a good decision.

Actively-managed funds have an advantage in that they can outperform the market, unlike index funds. This ability to beat the market attracts many investors to them. It makes sense to invest in them because you will receive the full market return, less the nominal fee you pay to the trader. However, history does not indicate that actively-managed funds will beat the performance of an index every time. It is also difficult for you as an individual investor to predict the performance of the indices correctly, and you could end up missing out or completely losing your investment when their performance plummets.

When you consider the issue of cost, actively-managed funds no longer take the lead because as we mentioned, the cost of managing them exceeds that of index funds. In fact, the issue of cost is a primary reason why index funds outperform actively-managed funds.

If you consider taxes, index funds will emerge more tax-efficient. The manager of an actively managed portfolio will trade more times than one trading index funds. The buying and selling, also called the turnover, leads to more taxable gains, so long as the funds are not placed in any of the special accounts we will talk about later on.

Comparing the strategies used, index funds buy all of the stocks in a particular index, indiscriminately. Actively-managed funds depend on thorough market studying, research, forecasting, experience, and expertise to select and manage a portfolio, thus the performance of actively-managed funds depend highly on their management teams. Choosing the right management team is not easy either.

Looking at the comparison above, each method has both strengths and weak points. You just have to make a choice and decide between long term earnings through index funds or short-term earnings brought by actively-managed funds.

Index Funds vs ETFs

As you go peeking at the index funds market or even reading about it, you are likely to come across exchange-traded funds, commonly known as ETFs. An ETF is a marketable security that follows an index, a product, bonds, or a bunch of assets, just like the index fund. However, unlike the index funds, it does not belong to the mutual funds family because it trades like normal stocks and securities on the security exchange. Its price fluctuates throughout the day as it is traded.

Index funds must strictly take the nature of mutual funds. Mutual funds have an end-of-day trading price at the end of each business day and traders are free to buy them at any amount of money, so long as it meets the minimum investment amount. The buyer is not also required to pay any commissions when purchasing mutual funds because representative trading companies like BlackRock, Vanguard, Fidelity, L &G, and HSBC trade them. Once the trading produces profits, these earnings are being ploughed back into the business and reinvested on your behalf.

Since an ETF is traded throughout the day, it is priced severally, and you will find that its price fluctuates all the time depending on the performance of the stock or the index, forces of demand and supply, and other factors that affect the financial markets. If you intend to invest in ETFs, you must monitor these price movements on the floor of the stock exchange market, just as traders who deal with stocks and shares do. Amazingly, you can start purchasing only one ETF because it does not have fractional shares like the index does. However, for ETFs, you will have to pay a commission, although most brokers are now offering commission-free ETFs.

Important to note, ETFs have a lower expense ratio than their counterparts, the index funds. For example, on the New York Stock Exchange Market, while the Vanguard Total Stock Market Index Fund Investor Shares mutual fund has a 0.14% expense ratio, the Vanguard Total Stock Market ETF only has a 0.04% expense ratio. That is ten basis points lower. You will also find that Admiral Shares of the same fund has an expense ratio similar to that of the ETF.

Because trading ETFs is similar to trading stocks, liquidating ETFs is easier and more tax efficient compared to index funds and other forms of mutual funds. In addition, when an investor decides to sell his ETF shares on the market, he will sell them directly to another investor seeking them in the market. However, when an investor decides to sell his mutual fund shares, the portfolio manager has the task and responsibility of raising the cash needed to pay out the investor, resulting in capital gains. Index funds are increasingly becoming popular, and portfolio managers have been able to increase the cash by taking it out of the money provided by new investors. However, as the market increasingly becomes crowded, this might change because there will be fewer entries and more exits, which means that companies will not have a flow of cash to pay the investors who cash out.

When trying to make a choice on which form of investment to take up, you would be safe investing in either of the two: ETFs and index funds because both have performed exceedingly well so far. By the beginning of 2014, 20.2 percent of all equity mutual fund assets in the United States were index funds. This growth came about because between the years 2007 and 2014, index-based exchange-traded funds (ETFs) and index domestic mutual funds received an additional $1 trillion cash that also included re-invested dividends. As a result, the ETFs have grown quite fast attracting twice the size of index domestic equity mutual funds, beginning in the year 2007. Conversely, actively-managed domestic equity mutual funds got a $659 billion outflow, inclusive of the reinvested dividends, in the same period.

Diversification of Index Funds

Diversity is the cornerstone of all investments, including index funds. You want to ensure that your investment is varied so that you are protected from the volatility of the market.

We have already established that index funds are inherently diverse because they are made up of an assortment of stocks and bonds. One index fund can hold a few hundred or even a few thousand companies. However, this diversity alone is not enough.

Like many other things in life, diversifying index funds is not really about the number of index funds you have, it is all about the quality of what you have. If you are holding multiple index funds of the same kind of stocks and bonds, you are not diversifying. However, if you buy an index that contains inventory from US-based companies and adds another that holds Non-US based stocks and bonds, you are broadening your prospects and lessening your risk. This now is diversification.

Most index funds focus on one particular market, like the Vanguard Total International Stock Market Index Fund that tracks index funds in emerging and developing markets outside of the United States. Vanguard advises long-term investors who would like to diversify their international portfolios to consider taking up this fund but buying a single type of fund will not offer you enough diversification. If you are looking to spread the risk evenly, consider taking index funds that follow both local and international portfolios. For example, instead of taking up American-based or UK-based index funds alone, take others based in China, Japan, or any other country.

One of the primary reasons for diversification of index funds is asset allocation. Asset allocation is the ability and tendency to balance investments across a number of categories including the national, international, value, or growth stocks. It makes sense to diversify the index funds across these asset classes. For example, you could purchase index funds that have large-cap U.S. value stock, large-cap U.S. growth stock, or an index fund for developing countries, and so on. It is possible to cut the slices into even smaller proportions for a more diverse allocation. You could also choose to buy multiple indices of the same asset class because each index will have its own unique rules, and many times, the rules do not clash.

However, there is a diversification limit; a limit on just how much diversification is of benefit to you. It is easy to make grand mistakes when trying to diversify, and at some point, the division of portions will be a waste of time. For example, you do not need five small-cap funds. Ideally, you can have US funds, international funds, income and growth funds, and funds from large to small companies, and that is all the diversification you will need. As long as your investment reflects variety, you are good to go.

At the end of the day, the amount of time you spend learning and researching will determine how well you can invest. Even when you are using the services of a broker, you should spend some considerable time researching by yourself. If you manage only to choose one index fund, it is also way better than not planning for your retirement at all. However, if you got the time, look around. Examine your portfolio, and you will reap great benefits in the future.

For beginners, it is best to seek the help and advice of a financial advisor or a broker who will show you a number of diversified investments that you can take up based on your risk tolerance, retirement goals, or other factors that are important, that guide your investment decisions. If you choose to handle everything by yourself, you may be overwhelmed and find difficulty deciding on the better indexes, and how to hedge against the risks that each brings.

Index Funds Are Ideal Long-Term Investments

You must have noticed that the word "retirement" was used occasionally when talking about investment in index funds. This is not by chance. By nature, investing, in itself, is not a quick strategy to make money. Sure, some investments will give some returns in just a short time, but they do not provide significant gains. Getting something meaningful from what you are investing in always demands commitment, patience, and that you keep calm even when the market fluctuates because inevitably, it does.

A long-term investment is likely to give you maximum returns in 10 years. Index funds are examples of such vehicles. On the other hand, you would only expect to hold a short-term investment for up to three years, before you can sell it and convert it to cash. Certificates of deposit, short-term bonds, and money market funds are examples of short-term investments. Day trading is also a risky venture that people engage in. However, for most people, long-term investment options are ideal because they are less stressful, and the returns are more stable.

As you invest in index funds, approach the market based on your preferred rate of return. Look for an index fund that averages your pre-determined rate of return in a five to ten-year period. Once you have invested, avoid panicking just because the value of the stock decreases, and avoid selling even when the market looks unfavorable. The market runs in a cycle and will always recover after a drop, although it may take a while to do so. If you sell your investment when the market decreases, and the prices are low, you risk losing a portion of your initial investment. Therefore, avoid looking at your portfolio often, sit tight and let the market forces do the work for you.

The longevity of the investment also determines the amount of risk you will be able to bear. The longer you are willing to invest your money, the bigger the risks your investment can take. If you need to collect your money in a few years, opt for a more conservative approach for investing, and lean towards more secure investments. Another determinant of the length of time to opt for is what you intend to use the money you will get for. This will also guide your decision because it will determine the amount of risk you are willing to bear.

In the end, index funds are best used as a long-term investment and are suitable for investment guided by a long-term goal such as retirement or as a way to secure money for college. Only avoid investing in a long-term investment and then selling it in just three years guided by a short-term goal like a dream vacation.

Take up the following tips when making long-term financial decisions:

1. The fundamental rule of investment is diversification. Always invest in different sectors of the market, balancing between high-risk high return investment such as stocks and lower risk stable return investment types.

2. Seek the services of a professional, a financial advisor, who will help you weigh out your financial goals against risk tolerance. A financial advisor will help you create an investment portfolio that takes into account your

unique factors. The set time you expect to receive your money will determine the risk you are willing to bear, and the amount of growth you desire.

3. When investing in a long-term financial goal, such as retirement or towards a college fund, the long-term investment should ideally start as risky, with a chance of getting a higher return and increasingly conservative over the years. For example, if you invest in a small-sized company, the beginning may be rocky as the company tries to establish itself in the market. However, with time, the company will grow and become one of the giants of the economy. You will be one of the greatest beneficiaries of this growth because the dividends will increase as the company expands and reaches a wider market.

Successful Index Fund Investors

As we proceed in the discussion of index funds investment, it is only right if you learn about various figures who have successfully invested in index funds, so you know that you are on the right track. Indeed, if you are going to take investment advice, you had better take it from a person who has succeeded at what he is advising you to do. Warren Buffet is one of the people who swear by the legitimacy of index funds as a successful investment vehicle. In the investment sphere, no one's wisdom is sought after more than that of Warren Buffet's. The chairman and CEO of Berkshire Hathaway was called the Oracle of Omaha because his comments on investments were followed by the community. Sure, we can learn a few tips from him.

The legendary investor made $1 million in 2007 in a bet he made against protégé partners. He bet that an S & P index would outperform hedge funds, and he won. His choice fund, the Vanguard 500 Index Fund Admiral Shares, had earned 7.1 percent returns compounded annually, while hedge funds his competitor had chosen only brought 2.2 percent. Each party had initially put in about $320,000 into bonds they expected would grow to become $1 million in a set period. However, since bonds appreciate much faster, they instead bought shares from Berkshire B. The returns of this entire deal would all go into charity, the partners agreed.

The results of this bet confirm Buffet's deep conviction that index funds are a smart investment choice, and that people should adopt it. Buffet particularly recommends index funds as a way to boost the savings you have kept for your retirement. He asks people to buy the S & P 500 low-cost index funds consistently. He also says that the trick is not in picking the right company but instead, to purchase shares of all big companies through the S & P 500 and to do it consistently. His advice makes so much sense because, for one, index funds are relatively inexpensive and are not tied to the success of only one company.

Buffet said that in investment, costs make a whole lot of difference. For example, if you expect 7 to 8 percent returns, then it makes sense if you spend 1 percent in management. The extra 6 or 7 percent will make an enormous difference in your retirement years.

In his 2017 annual letter to sharcholders, Warren gave pretty valuable yet straightforward advice. He asked both small and large investors to stick to investing in low-cost index funds reminding them that if they allow their money to be managed by the people at Wall Street, they will be charged high fees, and it is the managers that will reap the abnormal profits, and not the investors themselves.

This was not a new message from Buffet. In 2014, he gave similar advice to the trustees of his estate. He asked them to put 10 percent of all cash in short-term government bonds and the rest, 90%, in long-term, low-cost S & P index funds in the belief that the results from the long-term investment would be higher than that got from other forms of investment, and from that of investors who seek the services of money managers.

Buffet has a particularly grim view of financial managers, especially those that run hedge funds because they underperform the index in both the short- and the long-term.

Investors who have embraced Buffet's advice and taken up the index fund investment approach have come a long way. The Morningstar reported that when a number of investors fired their U.S.-based active managers in 2016, they brought in an extra $342.4 billion net from their funds. The proceeds, added to the new money brought in amounted to $505.6 billion, and this sum was immediately ushered into U.S.-based passively managed funds.

As of now, only a third of the investment money is held in passive exchange-traded and index funds, but this is bound to be dominant by the year 2024. Seeing this, the hedge fund industry is also throwing its punches by lowering its fees to attract wealthy investors and pensioners to invest in them. They are surely succeeding because these active funds sometimes beat the index. However, the point of having an index fund is to earn passively, which defeats the energy and time you are likely to use in your search for the perfect fund and the ideal manager who will bring in the high returns. Buffet said that the search for an ideal investment caused investors to waste a billion per year, money that could otherwise be invested in index funds.

Buffet is not the only one who supports index funds investment; self-made billionaire Mark Cuban also gives it the thumbs up. He advises investment beginners who do not know too much about the markets to start by investing in cheap S & P 500 index funds.

In his book "Unshakeable," Tony Robbins also talks about index funds and calls them the ultimate approach to passive income because they eliminate almost all activities of trade, reducing human error, and therefore taking out the risk that comes with picking stocks individually. He also adds that when you own an index fund, you are shielded from the biased, misguided and unlucky decisions that you or your fund managers are likely to make with time as you trade stocks.

Chapter 2: How to Invest in Index Funds

As you begin to dip your toes into the investment waters, it can be challenging to know where to go. You must have a ton of questions too, many of which lack a definite answer. If you intend to invest to cover future expenses or to secure your retirement, you are probably seeking out the best long-term investment method. Ideally, you want a method that will embrace diversity, one that will not distract you from your daily activities and one does not attract burdensome trading costs. In many ways, investing in index funds with the help of low-cost brokers will solve all these problems in one swoop! So, how do you go about it?

Here are the five critical steps that will guide you in this endeavor:

- Learn all there is to do with index funds and how they work
- Conduct an in-depth comparison of all the online brokerage companies available in terms of the fees charged and the functionality
- Consider adding ETFs to your index fund investment
- Only when you feel ready, open a trading account

- Buy index funds consistently and reinvest the dividends so that the funds grow and multiply themselves continually.

Index funds offer a fantastic stress-free strategy for building wealth that will get you started in your quest to venture deeper into the financial market. The learning curve is not as steep as most people imagine it to be because it is easy to open your own online brokerage account and to start investing immediately.

To start today, look up an online brokerage that offers a selection of index funds that you could be interested in. This is ideal for investors who want to cut out the middleman altogether. A Vanguard account, for example, would be ideal and easy to open. The company only asks for information on your checking account, but once you create the account, you can go ahead and start the business. Everything is managed electronically.

Almost all Vanguard accounts require an initial $3,000 to get to the fund directly or $1,000 as a Vanguard target date fund. The initial buy-in will surely have you saving all dimes and nickels you can find; you need to get your foot in. Vanguard offers invaluable tools that will allow you to make successive investments automatically such as allowing you to make investments each week or each month direct from your checking account, rolling up your dividends back to the index fund and others.

Taking the direct investment route is quite advantageous. For starters, the fees charged when investing directly are quite low, 0.1% to 0.2% of the principal investment fund, which is insignificant in comparison to the returns you expect from your investment.

Other people like to avoid the process themselves and instead, opt to use the services of a broker. There are a number of brokers in the market such as Schwab, TD Ameritrade, Ally Invest, and E*TRADE. The process of investing with them is similar to taking up the challenge yourself. You are asked to sign up with them online, provide details of your checking account and then start buying. Almost all brokerages charge a transaction fee for every buy or sell. Therefore, if by chance you sign up with TD Ameritrade and buy a Vanguard fund, you will be asked to pay Ameritrade's transaction fee for each sale or purchase, in addition to Vanguard's management fees.

In a situation like this, the solution is to purchase ETFs. The fees charged for ETFs are always lower than the amount that would be charged for an index fund of the same amount. For example, the Vanguard 500 index fund charges a 0.14% expense ratio or the management fees, while the SPDR 500 that tracks similar stock as an ETF only attracts a 0.0975% expense ratio.

Indeed, the key to making any investment is to move and get started immediately before life gets in the way; it tends to do that. The sooner you get your money growing and multiplying, the more time you give it for growth.

Below is a summary of the steps you should take when you want to go about investing in index funds.

1. Ensure that you can meet the minimum investment for your intended index funds.
Many index funds will require you to make an initial investment of between $2,000 and $3,000. This is the primary charge you pay to get the index funds, and once you have cleared it, you are free to start earning, although in small amounts. Each index fund will have a unique investment minimum, high or low. You only need to look through the market to identify one that is in your budget.

2. First, if you do not have a lot of starting capital, opt for an ETF index fund first.
Not having enough money ought not to stop you on your journey to securing your financial future; you can begin with an ETF fund. An ETF fund tracks the indexes of major companies like Google, Microsoft, and Apple on the S & P 500. These funds are a good bet because the

companies are stable, and it is likely that you will get a good return from them. In addition, the investment minimum for these companies is very low.

Going by this option is similar to index funds because you will not have to choose individual stocks; they are already classified and grouped.

If you can afford the investment minimum for index funds, go right ahead and buy, by yourself through either your account or a broker.

3. For a good return on investment, lean towards small-cap and mid-sized index funds. Index funds from these companies have more significant returns in the long run because the company itself is growing. However, spread out the risk by putting more of your funds on the mid-size index and less on the small-cap indexes.

4. Ensure that you create a diversified portfolio. An index funds investment can also be a portion of your larger investment portfolio. They help to strengthen your overall finances. In addition, ensure that the index funds themselves are diverse as discussed in chapter one above. Your broker, financial adviser, or the mutual fund company can offer you advice on how to add your new investment into the current portfolio, or how you can create a new diverse portfolio using index funds.

5. Ensure that the index on the funds is equal to or is close to the returns expected.
Companies trading index funds will have a quote page that shows the expected returns for the investment you make. There are also multiple quote pages online. Your broker could also provide you with one. Ensure that the index funds you intend to purchase on average have returns higher than the fees you will be paying. You should only invest in index funds whose returns completely cover the costs that will be charged. Also, make sure to avoid those that do not do well typically and those that offer the investors a constant return.

6. Opt for a brokerage company that has a variety of index funds.
Companies like Vanguard, State Street Global, and BlackRock are considered leaders in the index funds market, and they offer a wide range of index funds from which you can choose. Ensure that the company you are eyeing has the kind of index funds you are looking for before you commit to it. If you intend to make your investments in small amounts once you pay the minimum investment, opt for a mutual fund company because it does not impose any transaction fees for deposits.

7. One-time investments are best made through a broker.

Some brokers charge a transaction fee every time you input some money into your fund. If your choice broker does this, seek to make your investment as a lump sum, and if you have to add to it, only do so on rare occasions. This is also suitable for persons who operate using a personal brokerage account or for investors dealing with individual brokers instead of dealing with an established large mutual fund company.

Kindly also take note of the fact that some brokers also charge an additional processing fee for each transaction, while others will offer free trades for loyal clients.

8. Your banking information is required.
As you open an account or sign up with a mutual fund company, bank details, and a routing number are critical, and you will always be asked to provide them. Primary, these details are meant to provide a place where you will collect your returns from your investment. The broker or the mutual funds' company you select will also access your minimum investment from there.

In this, you are cautioned to only provide this sensitive information to brokers and companies you trust. If you are required to submit the information using the Internet, ensure that you are using a secure site and that the right protections have been installed.

9. Ensure that you pay all the fees linked to your index funds.
Typically, index funds attract fees but are often cheaper than stocks and other funds. Before you purchase any of them, look at the expense ratio for each. Most brokers and mutual fund companies often have broken down this cost into different kinds of fees. These fees should only be 0.1 percent or 0.2 percent of the principal amount to be invested. Compared to what you will make at the end of the investment period, this amount is negligible.

10. Pay up all the costs upfront.
It is necessary that you pay up the entire initial investment, the commissions, and any other associated fees upfront. Once you have done that, relax and watch as your returns flow back in.

11. It is essential to monitor the progress.
Just like any other investment, merely making a deposit is not enough; you need to keep an eye on what you have planted. Again, it is advisable not to do this too often, to avoid being stressed and discouraged when the index funds are not performing as expected. Typically, index funds are stable and will not change too radically, which takes out the need to monitor them all the time. It is okay to check on them at least one in a year to take note of the progress, so that you

may be assured that your investment is still secure and doing well.

Some people compare the progress of their index funds to that of others. The comparison helps you identify index funds that are doing much better than yours is. If you find that this is the case, you may switch to the one that is performing well after some years, increasing the returns.

12. Do not stop at the initial deposit.
Develop the habit of adding small amounts of money into your fund, possibly once every month, or several times in a year, to increase the principal amount and consequently your returns. In the event of a windfall or you find yourself with extra money after paying your bills, or you receive dividends from other investments, deposit the extra money into your fund. If your broker charges a transaction fee, reduce the number of times you make the deposits, opting for more substantial sums deposited few times instead of depositing small amounts every time you get them.

13. Trade non-performing index funds.
In the event, an index fund is consistently not performing as you were expecting, sell it through your broker or the mutual fund company. Beware that these dealers will charge a small fee, typically $10 per trade, but the non-

performing index funds will be out of your hands in the end.

In the event, you need the money you invested or would like to shift your investment, cash out! If you need the investment income to pay some bills or that you want to try out an alternative mutual fund or stocks, you may also cash out. Your broker or the company will aid in this process but will charge a small fee.

Chapter 3: How to Pick an Index Correctly

Everyone around you, including myself, is telling you to venture into index funds investment and to buy index funds as soon as possible. However, no one tells you how to pick the right one. This chapter discusses just that.

When it comes to selecting an index, there is no fast and hard rule to guide you, and this is the reason all investors should take extra caution when looking into the options available so that they can end up picking the best possible index fund. That said, some basic techniques could get you headed in the right direction. They include market capitalization weight, equal weight, and fundamental weight.

Market Capitalization

Beginning with the most popular of the three, market cap weighting categorizes the constituent stocks according to the market value of their outstanding shares. For example, in the real world, looking at the PowerShares NASDAQ 100 ETF, Apple Inc. (AAPL) takes up approximately 12.5% of the fund courtesy of its $500 billion market capitalization. In contrast, F5 Networks, the smallest holding, only takes up 0.17% because of its significantly lesser $7 billion market cap.

As you would expect, an index weighed in terms of capitalization will rise or decline dramatically as the company and its stock changes in value in comparison to other larger and smaller holdings. One benefit of this weighting style is that more stable and inherently larger companies will be more dominant than the small ones. The big companies absorb the volatility of the small ones.

Investors ought to take note of the fact that choosing cap-weighted indexes automatically and disproportionally tilts your equity allocation to the larger companies, which can inhibit the ability to monitor their performance over time. A recent study examined the stock market in 20 years and found that in reality, the small and mid-size cap stocks outperform the larger cap stocks by a significant margin and only present slightly higher volatility than that of larger cap stock.

Equal Weight Index

The same list of stock used to create market cap indexes is used to create equal weight indexes. However, instead of going ahead to examine the weight that each component stock exerts in an index, this method assigns an equal proportion to all securities. Therefore, using the same example, Apple Inc. will carry weight similar to F5 Networks.

On the surface, this method seems quite illogical compared to the market capitalization index method because investors seek to own a larger share of the established and successful companies. However, it makes more sense if the small and medium cap companies take a larger share of the pie in a growing market.

Let us use an actual situation that happened in 2013 to compare performances. It happened that the SPDR S & P 500 ETF (SPY) that is cap weighted earned 28.97% in gains. The equal-weighted Guggenheim S & P 500 ETF (RSP) earned 31.74%. This is a 2.77% variance. Comparing the accompanying expense ratios, RSP's is nearly four times that of SPS, at 0.40%. Even with a higher fee, equal weighting still makes for a compelling case.

It is also crucial for an investor to take note of the fact that smaller companies receive a larger share of the returns than large companies do because they are known to display a higher performance over time.

Fundamental Weight

This method of weighting is relatively new in comparison to the former two. In this method, the indexes are made to account for particular company metrics that can be compared across the spectrum such as earnings, book value, dividend rates, and revenue. Companies that present the most favorable front by exhibiting the strongest traits are assigned large weights in a particular index.

The advantage of this method is that companies receive merit purely based on performance and in this way, a company that has long been undervalued in the market gets recognition, and overvalued companies receive their due credit. This method also allows investors to review indexes based on metrics that are significant in business such as the free flow of cash. This metric is then compared to companies in the same sector.

Choosing the Right Index

The predominant theme that shows up from the evaluation of the three strategies discussed above is that the world is slowly shifting from methods that only favor largely established names and the smaller, nibbler, and profoundly sound companies are gaining recognition. The traits that are gradually being adopted are those that appeal to the investors who are seeking to invest in a stock that shows promise for the future. The investors should be aware, however, that this shift will undoubtedly come with accompanying increased volatility because the smaller companies are yet to stabilize.

That said, the process of selecting the right index to identify one that meets your personal needs adequately does not zero down to typical investment limitations like accessibility and size. Instead, your own goals and volatility tolerance make the difference. This is because investors are now adapted to traditional market capitalization weighting because it has been around longer. It is the reason why it should come down to your personal preference as you ask yourself whether you will be comfortable stepping out of the old approach of index funds investing to adopt a new fact-based approach.

The demand for newer, more specific and increasingly complex benchmarks is growing by the day, making index construction itself even more complicated. Investors are also making claims to index providers to use objective, transparent, rules-based and highest-quality techniques to develop indexes they are introducing to the market. To do this effectively, indexers are continuously scouting for data and matching technology that can make the indexing process as open and transparent enough for the traders, the product issuers and the investors. It is also easy to challenge the indexes created.

As the demand for alternative indexing strategies rises, it is essential for you to educate yourself on the intricacies to expect from the new products, and the benefits you should expect to reap from each. All this is meant to guide you in your selection and ultimately, allow you to choose a stable investment option. Investment rules emphasize on the need to perform due diligence on the investor's part and with that, with guidance from your personal goals, you should be able to select an index that is appropriate to your distinct investment needs.

Traits of an Excellent Index Fund

We have seen that index funds are judged and classified according to certain variables, which mcans that somc arc superior to others. Picking the wrong ones negatively affects your investment portfolio. Therefore, if you are looking to invest in them, you ought to examine each using a particular criterion that includes the following factors:

1. Does Not Have Narrow Funds

The reason you will find too many available index funds in the market is that a majority of them are not worth investing in. Although you may like to say to others that you now own individual shares, investing in an index fund that is confined to the holdings of a single country, for example, is just like picking stock, only that you are trying to time its performance, and you are paying an expense ratio to do only that.

2. Expenses Charged Should Be Low

Naturally, index funds are low-expense investment instruments, but mutual fund companies charge a 0.50% expense ratio or even higher. However, picking the index funds based on the fees the companies charge is ill-advised. However, ensuring that the costs are kept at a minimum guarantees higher returns and a more significant investment portfolio. See how you can balance the two.

3. Corresponds to the Primary Index

An index fund is no good if it does not correlate with the changes in the market. For example, if the value of your S & P 500 has risen in the market by 1% in a period of six months, yet your S & P Index fund has only risen by a 0.7% margin, then there is a significant correlation problem, possibly brought by the imposition of high fees that impede performance. It is unlikely that you will find a 100 % correlation, but the variances should not be significant either. Make sure to look out for the correlation history of the index funds over many years.

4. You Should Be Able to Understand the Index

Many experienced investors who have had experience picking their index funds understand the S & P 500 quite well. The S & P 500 is an index that represents 500 stocks, which is representative of a section of the economy. In this broad array of index funds, try to lean towards those that track indexes.

Overall, Bogle advocated for making an effort to keep the investment as simple as you can by taking out all variables that contain risks that you cannot control. The index funds already do this by eliminating a significant proportion of them by removing the need for picking stock, turnovers, money managers, and other expenses associated with actively-managed funds. He believed that trying to beat the economy by avoiding all kinds of risks also reduces the number of gains received over time.

The Psychology of Index Funds Investment

Index funds eliminate the need to take your time and effort in researching possible investments and having to manage the investment portfolio yourself. Moreover, another advantage they present is that they take out psychological biases that an investor needs to overcome to manage the investment portfolio effectively.

Beginning 1985 to 2015 that marks the end of 30 years, on average, an equity investor only gained a 3.66% annual return on average compared to the 10.35% average yearly return from S & P 500. How could you explain this huge variation? Why did the individual investors reap lower profits than those that used the S & P 500 index? The answer is quite simple; it is because of psychology.

In almost all occasions, individuals will use psychological bias to make decisions. Examples of psychological biases include:

Narrow framing: This is the practice of making decisions on what to invest in without considering the effect it will have on the total portfolio.

Loss aversion: Being loss averse is the fear of making losses, and it often causes the investors to sell their funds when the market is performing sub-optimally or when they prefer investing only in low-risk equities. In the end, the low risk only produces low returns.

Irrational optimism: It is okay to be hopeful about the market, but when an investor believes that only good things will happen to him as others enjoy losses, he is being irrationally optimistic.

Herding: Just as the name suggests, herding is following others blindly and copying their behavior, which often leads to poor investor behavior where they buy the index funds when they are selling high and selling when the price is low.

Anchoring: Anchoring is holding on to the past. It is the bias that occurs when an investor clings to the memories of the past instead of embracing and adapting the new market conditions.

Regret: Similar to anchoring, regret also deals with the past, where an investor allows the mistakes of the past influence present decision-making.

Mental accounting: Mental accounting is shared among investors who will take unnecessary risk in one investment area but avoid making a systematic risk in another area because the investor has separated his money into different segments in his mind. Not realizing that you failed to diversify: This is the tendency of investors to assume that their investment portfolios are quite diverse while in reality, the investor has invested in vastly correlated assets.

An index fund or a portfolio of index fund investments helps investors to mitigate the psychological constraints discussed above. An index fund is easy to purchase, maintain and produces returns similar to the returns of the index. Knowledge of these facts can significantly help an investor to quit being averse to risk and loss, and any other constraints that come up as investors are making an effort to build an investment portfolio.

Factoring in the Expense Ratio

Index funds are relatively cheap, have low expense ratios, do not attract high taxes, and will not generate many returns, particularly in the short-run. This does not mean that there will not be much eating into your returns. However, as stated earlier in the book, high fees significantly reduce the returns. To avoid getting into a trap like this, ensure that you factor in the expense ratios before you invest.

An expense ratio is the percentage of your investment fund that goes to the mutual fund company or the amount you use to pay the person managing your portfolio. The expense ratio can be as low as 0.03%, which means that for every $10,000 invested, a $3 is deducted in fees. The average expense ratio for his market, however, is 0.69% which means that for every $10,000 invested, the investing company will collect $69 in fees. These fees may look insignificant as of now, but when they add up, they may eat up all the returns.

Therefore, when considering index funds, even a slight difference in the expense ratios matters, especially when deciding on whether to seek the services of a broker or a financial advisor who could end up investing in actively-managed funds if left to make the investment decision. If this happens though, you will be forced to pay the higher expense ratio actively-managed funds attract, the higher taxes, and the financial advice fees. This does not mean hiring a financial advisor or a broker is a bad idea at all. However, keep in mind that index funds do not need constant monitoring and directing, and you could do just fine without hiring one.

Overall, it is clear that with index funds, you are more likely to direct more funds towards the investment rather than using a significant proportion of your funds to cover costs and expenses. Buffet calls these additional costs 'frictional costs' because an investor incurs that when he engages in buying and selling of stock occasionally. Buffet explained this concept further in his letter to Berkshire shareholders he wrote in 2005. In this letter, he told the story of the Gotrocks family, a family that had invested in almost all-American corporations. With time, the members of this family have hired "helpers" in the form of planners, brokers, and managers to help them grow their wealth, each member of the family competing against the others. However, as the family members hire more and more helpers, the family wealth is quickly shifting from the Gotrocks family to the helpers. Therefore, when dealing with investments, take care and ensure that the fees do not swallow up all the returns, and the principal investment.

Chapter 4: Buying the Index Funds

The process of buying an index fund is done in three simple steps. They are:

1. Making the decision on where to buy—this involves going through a list of brokers and their fund selection, factoring in the cost of the trade and seeing if there are options that do not require you to pay a commission.

2. Choosing a preferred index—choose a company to buy from based on the index it follows, whether the S & P or any other.

3. Looking at the investment income and other costs charged—this allows you to select the index fund and the brokerage company that suits your pocket.

The steps listed above are further discussed in this section below.

Step 1: Deciding Where You Want to Buy Your Index Funds

You have the choice of buying your index funds from a mutual fund company or seeking the services of a broker. This is also the case for persons purchasing ETFs although they are traded throughout the day, unlike index funds. When you are choosing between these options, ensure that you consider the following factors:

Convenience: get a funds provider who has the capacity to meet all your investment needs. For example, if you have decided to invest in mutual funds, and perhaps to add some stocks to it, the mutual fund company or the broker you choose should be able to provide you with both. They should act like a hub or a one-stop shop such that everything you may need is already available. For example, if you require screening tools and additional stock research, a discount broker who also offers index funds will provide you with personalized service delivery.

A selection of index funds: If you desire to purchase your index funds from different funds categories and families, a big mutual fund company should be able to provide you with a wide array of funds from which you can choose. However, although these companies are large, a discount broker will likely have a larger selection.

Is it Free? See if the providers you are eyeing for offer commission-free ETFs or free transactions for mutual funds. This criterion is used to rate brokers.

The costs of trading: Some brokers and mutual fund companies have scrapped off all transaction and commission fees, in a bid to please their current customers and attract new ones. However, others will still impose these fees. If you happen to lean towards one that imposes a fee, ensure that the fee is fair. Typically, you will be asked to pay $20 as a mutual fund commission or $10 if you are trading in ETFs and stocks.

Step 2: The Choice of an Index

Index funds are designed to track indexes, which makes it worthwhile to check out the indexes first before purchasing the funds. One of the very known indexes is the S & P 500 Index. It tracks 500 companies. Its portfolio is composed of popular, large, U.S.-based and other variations of companies. You can be sure that it represents a diverse industry spectrum. There are also other indexes, and they have attached index funds.

Each index has assets and stocks that are chosen based on certain basic criteria. Some of the factors considered when placing the companies in various indexes include:

Geography: stocks placed together based on geography are those that trade in the stock exchange market and other international exchanges.

Company's capitalization and size: Stock is differentiated based on the size of the company from which it is produced. It may include small, medium, or large companies.

The type of assets traded: Some funds track cash, others commodities, others domestic bonds while others concentrate on international bonds.

The size and the opportunities of the market they are from: The stocks could be from an established market, an emerging market or any other definition of a market.

The Industry or the business sector: Stock is drawn from companies that primarily focus on technology, consumer goods, fashion, healthcare services, hospitality, electronics, and other utility items.

Although the fund provider will provide you with an assortment and a variety of choices, you only need to invest in one. Buffet says that you only need to choose a broad stock and you will have sufficiently diversified.

You should also note that the index funds themselves are not rigid and you can come up with a customized allocation in case you want a selection that provides additional exposure in the market. For example, you may include more stock from emerging markets or increase the proportion given to small companies.

Step 3: Take Note of the Minimum Investment Requested, Among Other Costs

One of the highest selling points for any products, including index funds, is the cost of acquiring it. Low cost of purchasing and maintenance is particularly attractive to consumers, as opposed to high costs. Low-cost index funds are easier to run particularly because they are designed in such a way that they automatically follow in the steps of an index. This, however, does not mean that all index funds are cheap.

Although index funds do not need active management, they carry administrative costs that are subtracted from the returns of an investment. Two funds could carry the same investment goal, such as the need to track the S & P 500 index but their management costs could vary greatly. They may even differ by a fraction of a percentage point, and the difference may seem insignificant for now. However, in the long run, the small fee could take a toll on returns from the investment. Normally, a large fund attracts smaller fees.

Therefore, as you evaluate index funds, consider the following major costs:

The expense ratio: The expense ratio is one of the major costs that are taken out of the returns an investor is supposed to receive, often calculated as a percentage of the total amount invested. You should find the expense ratio in the prospectus or look it up in a financial site. Quoting some figures, the Investment Company Institute released in 2016 for context, stock index funds attract a 0.09% average annual expense ratio while bond index funds attract a 0.07% ratio. The expense ratio for an actively-managed stock is 0.82% while that of actively-managed bond funds stands at 0.58%.

Investment Minimum: This is the principal minimum amount a potential investor should have in his person when going out to purchase index funds. It is the minimum investment requirement, and as stated earlier on, it can rise to $3,000. Once the investor has met that threshold, he is allowed to continue investing, even in smaller amounts.

Tax-cost Ratio: Ownership of index funds attracts taxes that are imposed on all capital gains that are kept in checking accounts but for the IRA and the 401(k) accounts. Just like the expense ratio, the tax-cost ratio has a significant effect on investment returns. For many years, the tax-cost ratio has stood at 0.3% of all returns, although the rate can change.

Account Minimum: The account minimum is an entirely different concept from the investment minimum. While the minimum amount of money that can be in a brokerage account is $0, it does not mean that the investor is free to take out the investment minimum required for the specific index fund.

Other Important Considerations

Investors are increasingly taking up index funds as the choice method of investment for reasons like the ease of use, acquiring immediate diversity, and for their returns, which beat those of active funds with time. Therefore, as you put the final touches in your choice of index fund, here are a few other considerations to make and questions you can ask yourself.

Are you new to investing? If indeed you are new, get to learn the ropes of index funds investments. This book will comprehensively and adequately teach you all you need to know regarding this kind of investment

What type of investment do you intend to make? You need to make a decision on the type of investment which you would like to include in your portfolio. If you are seeking long-term growth, choose stocks and if you are looking for stability, pick bonds. If you already own either of the two, seek to balance the two. In addition, besides choosing between the bonds and the stocks, you need to decide on the level of diversification you intend to bring.

What are your financial goals? In answering this question, you ought to state what your main investment drive is. Some people save for retirement, others for a vacation in the future, while others invest in having available funds when their children join colleges. Whatever your goals are, ensure you invest in a fund that will make your money available at the time when you need it.

Are the index funds working as it should? The index funds you choose should replicate the index's performance. To ensure that this is the case, check its returns on the quote page. You should see the returns it has given in the past periods and compare this performance with that of the benchmark index. If the returns are close but not identical, do not panic because it is likely that they have also factored in the costs of managing the funds and the taxes. However, if the returns are lagging far behind by a margin bigger than the expense ratio, you ought to be alarmed.

Is the index fund you are targeting too expensive? If you are working with a tight budget, invest in ETFs instead, because they also track the index. Instead of just buying a small slice of the major mutual funds, start out with the ETFs, and you can purchase index funds later on.

Are there promotions running that you could take up? Sometimes brokerage firms offer promotions such as a cash bonus, or more. Although this should not be the predominant factor influencing your investment decision, it would be nice if you got to enjoy it.

Balancing and Rebalancing Index Investments

If you are yet to balance or rebalance your investment portfolio, it is possible that you have taken on too much risk that dissolves your diversification or you have leaned too heavily on a particular kind of investment type. It is also possible that your stocks are falling as your bonds rise, foreign stocks could be doing better than the domestic stocks, or small-cap stocks could be outperforming large-cap stocks.

Resetting the balance in cases like these requires you to ignore your emotions and preferences, sell off the most recent overachievers, and use that money to add onto the stock of the underachievers. Over time, you will see that it is ideal to sell your holdings when high and to buy when low. This process of selling and buying depending on the position of the stock is sometimes called the rebalancing bonus. Doing this may even add an entire percentage point to your annual average returns in the case of a long-term investment.

Rebalancing Methods

There are two principal methods of rebalancing a portfolio. Neither is more effective than the other, investors can choose either based on their preference. Each is easy to carry out especially if the stock in the portfolio had been chosen widely so that it represents clear asset classes.

    a. The As-Needed Method

In this method, you keep checking on your portfolio regularly and work to reestablish a balance when things are out of hand, even if it has only been a year, a month, a week, or a day since you rebalanced the portfolio. Carefully take note of the changes in your stock and take note of instances that require you to buy or sell some stock.

The As-Needed approach provides a large rebalancing bonus, but the associated high costs and the inevitable taxation eat up this bonus. It is also likely that an investor will lose on the momentum that sometimes allows securities to go higher than they should go.

b. The Calendar Approach

This method is quite common, and it involves changing the allocations in your portfolio going by the calendar. Many financial experts say that the ideal timing is at least after a year or 18 months, and many people prefer doing it after 18 months. However, if you are making money and living off your portfolio, you may want to make the changes more often so that it can continue making regular cash, perhaps every six months.

The calendar approach is of an advantage primarily because it gives you the discipline of sticking to a regular schedule. It also leads to lesser trading, which means that the fees and taxes that the transactions attract are low. This method also ensures that you are not there rebalancing all the time, which allows your portfolio to take a momentum that could drive your investment towards much profitability over time.

If you choose to take up this rebalancing approach, consider trading any part of your portfolio that has either grown by more than 10% away from the intended position or one that has shrunk by the same measure. This is to say that if your portfolio plan has a 20% to large-cap growth, you should sell or buy the portfolio if it falls short and gets to 18% or exceeds the limit and to get to 22%.

For someone who owns an ETF or a smaller portfolio rather than a mutual fund portfolio, try to stick to 15% instead of the common 10%. This is because the smaller a portfolio is, the smaller the positions, which means that your trading costs will be very high too. Certainly, you do not want to have to pay a whopping $10 just for trading a single index ETF worth $100.

The Best Time to Purchase Index Funds

Most seasoned index fund investors feel that there is not an appropriate time to invest in index funds; you just do it when you do it. However, it is important to take precaution by realizing that some market conditions will give index funds an upper hand over their counterparts, the actively-managed funds.

As you may have realized, the long-term investors are indifferent about timing because they do not have to worry about a thing. Once they have made their investment and bought index funds, they just have to wait for them to perform in the market and fetch them some returns. They do not have to worry about costs and other factors because index funds are inexpensive and easy to maintain by nature, the investors are assured that they will get decent returns. This is not the case for short-term investors.

Short-term investors who choose to invest in index funds have to employ short-term strategies such as looking out for the market conditions, and other factors that make the environment favorable for this kind of investment.

a. If you wish to trade in stocks, do it when the Bull Market is strong. The ideal time for selling stock is when prices are going up for all sectors, including the prices of different mutual fund types. At this time, it is easy to miss the trading window to major markets and active fund managers must move fast to match or even beat them. For example, in 2006, the market was in the final calendar year run of the current Bull Run, and the Vanguard 500 Index was able to beat more than three-quarters of the larger blend funds. The same happened in the years 2010 and 2011 when the stocks had fully recovered from the 2008 financial crisis, and the Vanguard 500 Index beat 70% and 80% of its peers yet again.

b. When the economic conditions are weak, it is time to trade bonds. Navigating a bond market may prove difficult, and fund managers who deal with actively-managed funds especially find it rough because they lose to index funds such as the Vanguard Total Bond Market Index (VBMFX). For example, this happened in 2011 when the economy slipped a bit during recovery. Bond funds had a positive year, and stock funds were also quite lucky because they were able to evade the negative returns. In fact, the VBMFX rose higher than 85% of all other intermediate-term bond funds.

It is also quite important for you to note that index funds are more likely to lose to actively-managed fund when the markets are volatile. They are less likely to do well in this environment, but an active fund manager will sift through the bonds or the stocks and end up outperforming even the major market indices. A market with such an environment is often called a stock-picker's market.

Kindly also note that just like any other markets, there will be some stocks or bonds that will perform better than others, even in a volatile market will.

So, Really, When Should You Buy?

It is normal to get anxious especially about when to conduct the initial purchase because starting at the wrong point could bring you big losses in the nick of time. However, you can take your heart from it because when you invest in index funds, time will favor you. Even if you experience a loss at first, the compounding returns you will get with time, assuming that you have picked the right fund, will add up and result in great profits.

Therefore, when you perceive that you want to invest in index funds, avoid wasting time! Instead of pacing around worrying about when to dip your feet in, think first, about the length of time you hope to keep the money there. Different kinds of investments will have different kinds of returns and risks, and each has an ideal period it should stay in the market.

Generally, if you go for bonds-based funds, expect smaller but dependable returns over a short period. Between the years 1926 and 2003 (2003 marked the end of a bear market), United States Treasury bills brought in 3.7% annually. Although this may seem like a small margin, remember that most of that period, there was no inflation, which makes the 3.7% annual return very attractive for that time. Government bonds that have lasted a longer period have always given a higher return. In the same period, 1926 to 2003, they gave a 5.4% average annual return.

Stock-based funds have also been of benefit to investors. Looking at the 1926 to 2003 period again, large-cap stocks gave an average 10.4% each year, which was significantly higher than the bonds.

Overall, the longer time you amass your money, the more you open yourself up to greater risks because you allow it to wait out even in periods of bad returns. It all boils down, however, to when you need your money back.

If you plan on cashing out after five years, avoid stock-centric mutual funds, and do not even attempt to purchase individual stocks. If you will cash out after three years, walk away from real estate investment trusts and bond mutual funds because they can drop once the interest rates go up.

When Should You Sell?

Once you have passed the big hurdle of deciding on the right index funds to purchase, and when to buy it, the next step is to determine the exact time you will cash out. Bonds sell themselves when they mature, which means that the question on when to sell applies only to stock-based mutual funds.

Some investors are convinced that they have the ability to accurately "time" the market by running an accurate prediction of when the market will rise and when it shall fall. This makes them avoid selling their stocks at a time when the market is about to fall and buying the stock back when the market is rising. However, if investing was as easy as that, these people would now be millionaires and billionaires. The reality is that as soon as the economic forces start to affect corporate earnings negatively, and companies begin to struggle, it is acceptable to start selling stock from overvalued yet low-quality companies. Aside from that, having an accurate timing system to guide you in the market will remain a dream.

Most investors, however, rush to take out their investments when the returns start turning sour. However, history and research had shown that investors who keep shifting camp from one index fund to another, in the pursuit of performance end up far worse than those who stayed when the luck changed. Therefore, when you purchase an index fund, prepare to stick by it through its performance, whether good or bad.

There is one exception, however, and although it deals with active funds. This tip could help you in your investment decisions when trying to make a choice between actively-managed funds and index funds. Investors who have entrusted their investments to a funds' manager who realize that the manager has now shifted from their funds to managing another client should not seek the services of a new manager. It is likely that he or she may not be able to keep the pace of the former manager, and therefore, the most feasible solution, in this case, is to sell. Otherwise, if your funds have been performing poorly for a few months, don't think of jumping ship yet.

While we are yet on the subject of selling, there are other two reasons for selling that have to do with stocks that could affect your stock-based funds. These should act as warning signs, and once you see either of the two, know that it is time to sell.

The first is when you realize that a business is changing its fundamentals. It could be that new competition has come up and it is rendering the company's central products obsolete. It could also be that the company is shifting from its core business and going into other areas that have nothing to do with its core competencies, and you can no longer understand what the business is all about.

The second warning sign is the overvaluing of stock. You know that a stock is overvalued by looking at signals like the earnings yield. If the yields exceed the earnings yield by 3 to 1, the stock is overvalued. Avoid investing in companies whose stock has a price-to-earnings ratio greater than the average growth rate. The company should also be producing products that customers want. If a company has high returns and this growth is not reflected by high consumer demand, the stock is overvalued. Stock like this is likely to crash at the slightest trigger. However, also find out whether the weight of a tumble could exceed what you would have to pay in taxes if you sold the company's stocks right now.

A Summary

There isn't an agreed on or a perfect time or rule that governs investments in index funds but for the common mantra: buy low, sell high and since you do not own a magic crystal ball that will tell you when to buy the index fund, the time is now. This is because the more time your money spends in the stock market, the larger it grows.

Therefore, if you invest today, your money begins to grow today courtesy of the compound interest magic. Compound interest causes your money to grow very fast because it continuously cultivates even the annual returns. You will be earning interest on your principal investment and your interest. Here's an example the New York Times gave to prove this.

Let's say a person commits to investing $5000 annually, and the money earns a 6 percent interest return per year; if the person starts doing this at the age of 32, by the time the person is 67 years, he will have $557,173.80. Suppose the individual had started 10 years earlier when he was 22 years, the money will have grown to $1,063,717.57. By starting the process earlier, the person will have earned twice as much.

In regard to how you invest, you mainly have two options, each with its own risk level. You only choose the level you are comfortable with. The first, dollar-cost averaging is a conservative one. It requires you to invest a fixed amount occasionally, just like in the example above. The idea behind this method is to cut down on investment risks that cause daily market fluctuations. The second option is to make your entire investment in one lump-sum instead of putting it in smaller amounts.

There is no consensus on which the better option is, but Vanguard study done in 2016 to analyze major market indexes from way back in 1926 showed that investing in a lump-sum is way better than dollar-cost averaging; on average, it beats it 2 out of 3 times.

Looking at lump-sum investments practically, it may be difficult for most people to save large sums of money, life being what it is. Even if you did and purchased your funds during a high, a dip would cause you too much regret and possibly send you into a panic mode, and you might end up selling again. Therefore, choose an investment method when you are sure that you can handle the risks that come with it, and remain calm no matter what happens.

Here are some tips to help you determine the length of time you should opt for while investing:

1. When investing, you have the choice of picking either bonds or stocks. If you are young and perceive that it will take you a long time before you need the money, predominantly by stock index funds. These carry more risk in the short term.
2. If you want to avoid too much risk, which is the case for people who are nearing the retirement age, consider taking up bond index funds because they are less influenced by the rise and fall of the market.

If you think this step-by-step guide is useful, feel free to leave a review in Amazon and let us know what you think about it.

Chapter 5: The Best Index Funds and the Best Mutual Fund Companies

An index fund is considered most favorable or the best if its expenses are low and if it contains a diversified portfolio that is stable and can stand much of the changes that happen in the market. Since there is a wide variety from which to choose, it is important that we pick a few of the best, to ease your selection and boost your knowledge of the market.

Lately, a large number of ETFs and index funds have hit the market, and although many of them are from familiar companies and look favorable, they really are not. Majority of them focus on narrow economy sectors such as social media, biotechnology, or Master Limited Partnerships (MLPs). These narrow funds can bring you very high returns in the short-term, but they are also prone to very significant declines. They also impose very high expense ratios compared to others in the market.

The ideal index fund, however, is one that is cheap, and diverse. Below are some that fit this criterion:

The Best S & P 500 Index Funds

The S & P 500 Index is one of the most popular index funds. It is based on stocks drawn from some of the largest American companies, each measured by capitalization. Some of them include:

The Vanguard 500 Index (VFINX)

The Vanguard 500 Index is a special pioneer index because it is the first index fund that the public can take up. Jack Bogle created it after observing the markets and noticing that any professional portfolio managers and individual investors were unable to beat market averages in the long-run especially after subtracting their costs. Bogle reasoned that if the investors were able to buy a low-cost mutual fund as a bunch of stocks packaged in an index, the investors could reap reasonable returns. He then came up with VFINX which requires $3,000 as the minimum initial investment and attracts a 0.16 expense ratio.

Schwab S & P 500 Index Fund

Charles Schwab, through his company, The Charles Schwab Corporation created the Schwab S & P 500 Index (quite a number of Schwab). This SWPPX is a mutual fund that seeks to provide more than just a discounted brokerage service to investors. This fund has established itself in the market in an effort to compete with big companies like Fidelity and Vanguard. In fact, it recently lowered its expense ratio, which now stands at 0.03%. Its minimum initial investment is a mere $100.

Fidelity Spartan 500 Index (FUSEX)

The Fidelity Spartan 500 Index is issued by the company, Fidelity. Fidelity has long been in the market since 1988, size and the desire to compete with other large providers like Vanguard has the company providing one of the lowest-cost and diverse large-cap indexes. Sometimes, it is difficult to distinguish between Vanguard and Fidelity because the companies are similar in terms of performance and expenses. This competition is of benefit to the investors because it provides indexes of the highest quality. Fidelity's minimum initial investment is $2,500 while its expense ratio is a mere 0.10 %.

T. Rowe Price Equity Index 500 Fund

Abbreviated as PREIX, this index fund was launched into the market in 1990, and since then, it has maintained one of the top return rates at 9.5%. The fund seeks to match the performance of large-cap stocks with that of its benchmark index. PREIX has a 0.21% expense ratio.

Best Aggressive Stock Index Funds

Aggressive stock is attractive to investors who are not shaken by short-term market changes. The investor can withstand seeing the market fluctuate and his account balance moving up and down as the investment climate changes, at least, in the short term. If this describes you, the following index funds are suitable for you.

Fidelity NASDAQ Composite Index

Abbreviated as FNCMX, this NASDAQ Index is mainly made up of large-cap stocks particularly those drawn from the health and the technology industry because they have greater growth potential in the long-term than other broader market indexes. Therefore, if the added risk of having a long-term index and getting higher returns in the process, then FNCMX is for you. Its expense ratio is 0.29% and $2,500 as the minimum initial investment.

Vanguard Growth Index (VIGRX)

The VICRX invests in large-cap stocks but only in those that still have a potential for growth. This makes it a little riskier but also increases its potential to produce greater rewards in the long run in comparison to other S & P 500 Index Funds. The minimum initial investment an individual can make is $3,000 and pays an attached 0.22% expense ratio.

Vanguard Mid-Cap Index (VIMSX)

Many experts agree that the best chance an investor could have at beating the S & P 500 Index is by purchasing an index fund based on mid-cap stocks whose performance history is better than that of large-cap stocks. In addition, the risk is less when holding mid-cap stocks than when holding small-cap stocks. This makes the VIMSX an exception, and therefore, when you do get it, you automatically land the 'sweet spot' of investing. It comes with higher returns and relatively lower risks. The minimum initial investment for VIMSX is $3,000, and its expense ratio is 0.20%.

The Best Bond Index Funds

Every investor can achieve a diversified portfolio courtesy of bonds. Index funds and other mutual funds are an ideal way to capture the extensive bond market in a single buy. The total bond market index often refers to ETFs and index mutual funds that have invested in the Barclay's Aggregate Bond Index, also called the BarCap Aggregate. This BarCap Aggregate is an extensive bond index that covers almost all bonds traded in the United States and a few foreign bonds that allowed into the U.S. market. Some of the best of these kinds of bonds include:

Fidelity Total Bond

This index fund is abbreviated as FTBFX and is broadly diversified, just like that of Vanguard, the VBMFX. However, this one is more flexible and capable of balancing both rewards and risks. This means that the FTBFX can hold many high-yield bonds and could capture greater returns in the long-term in comparison to the VBMFX. The minimum initial investment for this fund is $2,500 while the expense ratio is 0.45%.

Vanguard Total Bond Market Index

This is the VBMFX mentioned above. It is the largest bond index fund across the globe, having the largest collection of assets being managed. It is preferred by DIY (Do It Yourself) investors and the majority of managers who do not ask for commissions but fees alone.

When you purchase this bond, you have direct access to the entire bond market of the United States, which contains thousands of bonds, from corporate, short-term, treasury, intermediate-term, long-term and other kinds of bonds. The minimum investment ratio for this bond is $3,000, and its expense ratio is 0.16%.

The Best-Balanced Index Fund

A balanced index fund provides you with a simple way of having a diverse mixture of both bonds and stocks in a single index. The best-balanced index fund is the Vanguard Balanced Index, the VBINX. This fund balances the risks and the rewards in an excellent way while keeping the costs very low, in the long term. The allocation of assets is maintained at 40% bonds and 60% stocks which makes it an excellent pick for investors who seek a medium risk investment. Reviewing its returns for a 15-year period up through to 2016, you can see that its long-term returns have been attractive at 7%. The minimum initial investment for this fund is $3,000 while its expense ratio is a low 0.22%.

Although there are other balanced index funds, this one stands out.

Index Funds You Can Hold Forever

Warren Buffet once said that his ideal holding period for a fund is forever. The word forever in this statement raised questions regarding the index funds that an investor can hold for a long time. Traditionally, index funds are an ideal 'set it and forget it' solution because it cuts various costs and even eliminates the intermediaries. Some of the best lifetime funds include:

iShares Core S & P Total US Stock Market Index (iTOT)

The iTOT is an excellent fund to have forever because it is quite diverse, and its costs are quite low. This fund has a 0.03 % annual expense ratio, which means that for every $10,000 you invest, you pay $3 as fees. This fund owns nearly all stocks in the U.S. market and this means that you will not have to scout the market trying to pick a mixture of large, mid and small-cap stocks because, with just this single bond, you now own almost all kinds of stock in the market.

A very broadly diversified portfolio is advantageous because running it is very efficient especially when the portfolio has been weighed to determine the market cap before. Once you get there, the stock weightings will determine the price to be paid and make some adjustments as the market flows.

Since this fund cuts across almost all kinds of stock, it increases the number of risks it faces. First, it will feel the bear market's full force, but this also guarantees that it will not miss a single rally. (The bear market is the period when the prices of stock fall, causing the investors' confidence to be too low.) For example, in October 2007 during the bear market, up to March the next year, this fund lost more than the average losses faced by the large-blend category. However, when the markets started to recover, it recovered quicker than all the other funds because it took in the entire rally. That said, this fund is still highly ranked, efficient, cheap, and a great quick way to own the entire United States stock market.

Broad Bond Market Index Fund

Investors who are particularly interested in bonds can reasonably invest in the Broad Bond Market Index Fund and walk, although funds that focus on the Bloomberg Barclays Aggregate Index largely emphasize on government bonds. Those opting for an actively-managed solution can take up actively-managed bond funds that have stable management and sensible strategies because they too are an excellent forever fund.

One of the best core long-term holding bonds is Dodge & Cox. This fund stands out, first, because of its experienced and stable management team. The team approach, in this case, reduces the risk of management turnover, and if it does happen, it's less chaotic. Investors who choose this holding do not have to wonder about their choices.

Parent is also another great holding that you can lean towards. In this one, the management makes its investments alongside those of its customers, which is reassuring. The team takes a value-based long-term approach that favors corporate bonds, and the team is quite open to risks, sometimes venturing into the downtrodden controversial parts of the market to ensure that their investors are getting something. However, this holding is quick to take off its hold on valuations that do not show promise, which is something good about them.

Overall, the all-inclusive index fund that contains both stocks and bonds is an excellent choice for investors who desire to spread their risks to both stocks and bonds without having to constantly worry or manage the investment. The key to selecting the right fund is by ensuring that the holding firm is good at managing both bond and stock investments.

The Best Total Market Index Funds

Total market index funds comprise of both ETFs and mutual funds that take up a particular equity index as a benchmark. When it invests in the stocks of its benchmark index, this fund's portfolio performance seeks to ape the performance of the index, at least before the expenses and fees are imposed.

Typically, these funds are held by domestic U.S. stocks of major popular corporations and by the companies that are lesser known and have a small market capitalization. The total market index fund manages a number of those small public companies not traded leading to high costs of the transaction and high trading spreads but these.

Overall, the total stock market index funds contain a large number of equities and offer one of the widest diversifications an investor can get within the United States equity market. The 2000s have seen a massive increase in this kind of index funds, and here are some of the best in the market.

Schwab Total Stock Market Index Fund (SWTSX)

The Schwab Total Stock Market Index Fund keeps track of the total return of the United States equity market in its entirety as measured by the Dow Jones United States Total Stock Market Index. Currently, the SWTSX focuses more on sectors that have to do with financial services, technology, healthcare, industrial sectors, and the cyclical consumer. Of its portfolio, large market cap stocks take up 70%. It matches its top five holding to those of the Vanguard, and they take up the same proportion of its portfolio, 11.7%.

In ten years, 2008 to 2018, the fund generated an average 12% annual return, beating its benchmark that stood at 10.8% return. This fund does not charge any initial commissions and has a low expense ratio of 0.05%. It suits investors who desire total market exposure without having to pay much in expenses.

Vanguard Total Stock Market Index (VTSMX)

This index fund tracks the performance of the CRSP U.S. Total Market Index that is made up of investable U.S. stock drawn from different companies, of different market capitalizations that are traded on the NASDAQ and on the New York Stock Exchange.

The VTSMX mainly deals with companies in the technology, healthcare, financial services, industrial companies, and consumer cyclical sectors. Large market cap companies take up at least 70% of the assets, medium companies take up 19% of the portfolio, while small companies take up 9%, which makes this portfolio well diversified. The top five holdings, which include Microsoft Corp., Berkshire Hathaway, Apple, Inc., Amazon.com, and Facebook take up 11.7% of the total assets invested.

In ten years, from 2008 to 2018, this fund has generated 11.96% annual average returns while its benchmark had a 12.08% returns rate. Its expense ratio is 0.14%. This fund is best suited for investors who want to learn more on the financial services and the technology sectors, with the right exposure of a diverse portfolio and the benefits of a low expense ratio.

iShares Russel 3000

The iShares Russel 3000 is an ETF that tracks the Russel 3000 index, which indicates the investment results of the broader United States equity market. This fund uses the indexing approach and uses a sample of stocks to represent the benchmark beneath. This fund's sector allocations are quite similar to those of the Schwab and Vanguard, and the top five holdings make up 12% of its portfolio. In addition, 75% of the fund's assets are in large-cap companies.

In the ten years between 2008 and 2018, this fund produced an 11.8% annual average return. Its expense ratio stands at 0.2%, which doubles that of the Schwab Total Stock Market Index Fund. This fund is suitable for investors who are passionate about the Russell 3000 index and would not mind paying the slightly higher fees.

Wilshire 5000 Index Investment Fund (WFIVX)

This mutual fund tracks the Wilshire 5000 Index, an index weighed based on market capitalization, based on the market value of actively traded stocks of companies with their headquarters in the United States. Although the Wilshire 5000 Index has stock from 3600 companies, the fund only holds 1000 to 2500 of them, emphasizing on large-cap companies.

They account for 74% of the fund's portfolio. The rest, the medium and small-cap companies, are allotted 18% and 8% of the allocation, respectively.

The fund lays more emphasis on sectors similar to its competitors, which includes technology, healthcare, financial services, industrial, and cyclical consumer sectors. Surprisingly, its top five holdings are only allocated a 14% share of the entire portfolio. This fund also comes with an unusually steep expense ratio of 0.63%. Investors who have an interest in the performance of the Wilshire 5000 Index but do not mind the steep fees should surely invest in this index fund.

If you are wondering what the top 10 index funds are, do not forget to claim your bonus at the end of the book. The Index Funds Kickstarter bonus includes 10-year performance, total assets, expense ratio and also 1-year performance.

Chapter 6: Tax Considerations

Many investors do not stop to consider just what a significant issue taxes can be especially in regard to their long-term investments and returns. In a survey, a thousand respondents who have mutual fund investments were asked questions to test their knowledge of taxes. 85% of the sample confirmed that they were aware of the influence that taxes have on investment decisions. Those that showed a satisfactory understanding of implications that taxes have on investments were only 33%. In addition, 82% could not tell what the maximum tax rate was implied on long-term returns.

In truth, taxes can be a significant factor in regard to dividends, capital gains, and interest. Experts estimate that on average, an investor dealing with active mutual funds loses at least 3% of his returns every year through taxation. In fact, the more the earnings through active mutual funds, the more the taxes to be paid. This deduction is detrimental to the process of making wealth, and overall, it beats the point of investing.

A certain university conducted a study to measure the performance of 62 different equity funds for the period between 1963 and 1992. The study found that each dollar invested in this financial vehicle had the potential of growing and getting to $21.89 if kept in a tax-deferred account. When invested in a taxable account, the same dollar had the potential of growing and getting to a mere $9.87. Both cases considered an investor in a high-tax bracket. The group of researchers found that on average, tax reduces returns by 57.5%. Index funds are a little different though, because of their low portfolio turnover and the very low capital gains distribution. These two factors reduce taxation significantly—however, a key factor influencing investment decisions.

Fund managers dealing with active funds are not easily alarmed by taxation in the management of investments. This is because their evaluation and rating are done on pre-tax returns, which means that they lack any incentive to pay attention to how the taxes affect their trading, which is your investment. Therefore, do not allow the rating of a financial manager to lure you into thinking that his management of active funds is similar to that of index funds. Many of them do not regard the high taxes your stock will pick or the market timing, or the performance of the funds they are handling. It is also important for you to note that in your evaluation of these managers, you will also not find the taxes imposed on realized capital gains on the charts depicting the performance of the active mutual fund. However, these are pushed along further down and will eventually catch the investor by surprise.

Taxes Should Matter

Among the reasons many people prefer investing in index-based mutual funds and ETFs is the fact that they attract fewer taxes as we have mentioned earlier. This means that the amount paid in annual taxes is smaller than that paid when dealing with actively-managed funds.

However, some index products are less tax efficient than others, and on occasion, those who have invested in a number of them will bc blindsided by substantial tax bills. Once you have decided to invest in index funds, it is prudent for you to keep an eye out in the market, looking out for the ones that could surprise you with a hefty bill. In most cases, the ones that come with an overly large end of year bonus have attracted the big tax bills.

By the leading of the Federal Law, all net capital gains from holdings that were sold in a particular year must be paid out in distributions that are commonly issued in December. Unless the funds are held in a tax-deferred account such as a 401(k) or an individual retirement account, both short-term and long-term gains are subject to taxation. Index funds that lean towards the creation of income such as real estate investment trusts, bond funds, and high dividend payers also attract tax bill although the revenue flows in throughout the year and is not given as an end of year single distribution.

Therefore, investors who are intent on pursuing tax efficiency should focus their divided funds towards tax-sheltered accounts like the 401(k)s and the IRAs or stick to the plain-vanilla broad-market index funds and ETFs.

UK index fund investors have to pay taxes at 28% of their total capital gains if the combination of taxable gains and income goes beyond the income tax basic rate band. If the earnings are below that rate, then the taxation rates drop to 18% of the capital gains. However, individuals can enjoy an annual tax allowance of 11,700 euros as at the 2018/19 financial year. This allowance is meant to encourage investors to invest. To acquire information about the taxation rates used in other countries, kindly look through the government taxation websites. Each country will have unique taxation rates and possible exemptions.

Typically, index products do not support significant distributions because the assets they hold have an underlying index for the long-term. Therefore, if a stock in the index fund goes up, it increases the share price of the entire fund, or better yet, its net asset value. The investor will gain benefits in the end because the share price will be up. Although the gains will be taxed at that point and will need to be paid immediately, the sale of the index fund itself can be postponed for many years as the returns continue helping to boost and to compound the fund, with time.

Having learned that, you must be asking the question: How then are the indexers that give large distributions at the end of the year does it? The answer is here. In many cases, the indexers raise this capital from the sale of index fund holdings when they need to raise money that will be paid to investors who have decided to redeem their investments.

We have already learned that a low turnover makes the index funds investment to have small distributions. However, this also is dependent on the underlying index having a low turnover too. Therefore, if a provider of commercial benchmarks informs an index manager that a particular number of stocks is being added to an index and a certain amount of another stock is to be deleted from the said index, the index manager has to purchase and sell the stocks. This is another avenue for increasing capital gains. This is commonly done for small-cap indexes.

Index funds tracking bonds, particularly the shorter bonds, tend to have a high turnover because they have to continually take out the bonds that have matured or those close to maturity and replace them with others. The pickier a manager is about the membership, and the more frequent the manager will need to keep replacing the mature holdings. An increase in activity is likely to attract more taxes.

ETFs are also quite tax efficient because they do not need to sell the stock when the need for money arises such as when paying redemptions. When an ETF investor wants out, he only has to sell his holding on the stock market, just as if they were dealing with common stock. However, as part of the ETF framework, big investors, often referred to as authorized participants, are paid off in securities instead of cash when they want out. This is because their participation helps ETFs to create new shares and retire old ones as the demand changes.

Precaution Against Huge Taxes

Below are a number of steps you can take up to avoid investing in funds that attract huge taxes:

First, opt for an ETF alternative in place of your traditional indexed mutual fund. Keep off all kinds of index funds that have in the past paid very large distributions in comparison to their competitors. This is a sign that something fishy is driving them to do things as they are doing them, to bury something, and this might as well happen again.

Review the catalogs and other index fund material provided, and look for comments from existing customers on the tax efficiency of the bonds they have invested in. Beware that some index managers employ some weird techniques to reduce their distributions using techniques such as putting high-cost shares up for sale instead of cutting back on some holdings.

Take note of or rather, keep away from ETFs and index funds that tend to be too fancy by including new features like betting and leverage on derivatives. Techniques like these are meant to increase boost and modify the earnings of their holdings beyond the performance of the underlying index so that the managers can give out big distributions or be able to afford to pay out many redemptions in the event things do not go as expected.

Avoid index funds whose expense ratio is higher than that of similar indexers of the same category because the high fees could increase the number of redemptions.

Do not purchase a mutual fund that nears its dividend date because you will be asked to pay taxes for the gains and the income that was earned throughout the year. If you do, you will be buying a bill. In addition, once the fund has paid out the distributions, the price of its shares drops by the amount that has been remitted. Therefore, when you buy the index funds close to the payout, you will not be getting anything extra because the distribution will have been factored in the price of the shares.

Another way to reduce taxes is by harvesting losses if your distribution is large enough to allow it. Harvesting losses is a polite term that refers to the discriminatory behavior of selling all the index fund shares that are performing dismally. Sum up all the long-term losses of the past to determine which shares will go, to take off pressure on the long-term gains of the fund. In the event the losses are more than the gains, deduct a maximum $3000 from your income to cover them. Once you have done that and still have losses left, carry the rest over, and you can deduct them in the next year. Taking out the losing fund is advisable, especially because it affects taxation. However, the driving force behind this should be to improve the performance of your index and not to evade taxes. Taxes should always be a secondary consideration when trying to line up the stock in your portfolio.

While this last one might be blasphemous, it could be of benefit to an investor having trouble with index funds investment. However, as a last resort, you could also consider taking up an actively-managed fund that minimizes both takes and the number of distributions made. The kind that seeks to lower its taxes, also called tax-managed funds, take up all kinds of strategies, such as postponing sales to increase capital gains, offsetting the gains of winners by selling to losers, and even selling the high-value holdings to trigger even the smallest taxable gains.

Chapter 7: Advantages of Index Fund Investment

Here are the advantages of owning index funds:

Index Funds Are Managed Passively

There are two ways to manage mutual funds: actively or passively. An actively-managed fund requires a manager who will work continuously to ensure that he is beating the market. This carries a lot of risks because occasionally, the manager will make the wrong decisions, and sometimes, the stock will not perform as expected. The performance of the fund depends on the performance of the manager. Conversely, a passively-managed index fund only requires the manager to buy and maintain the securities of a given index so that they match the performance of the underlying index. He does not work to beat it.

Suitable for Beginners in Investment

This investment option suits beginners and inexperienced investors who may not know much about index funds or other forms of investment. In fact, it does not require prior knowledge about investing because you learn on the "job." As you invest occasionally, a know-nothing investor will gain so much knowledge, even better than the professionals themselves. This belief has often found resistance from some traditional investors who insist that investing in index funds and that a person who wants to learn the trade should begin by investing in an active portfolio both for the returns and for the experience. They believe that if you keep interacting with your portfolio as you learn from fund managers, you are likely to learn faster.

The gist of the matter, however, is that for a beginner to learn how to outsmart the market, so much work, learning and time are needed. Not many have the time to do this, and it is actually off-putting. Most investors would agree. While having an idea about what you are doing and what to expect is important, not everyone can become a professional, we are living in the age of specialization and outsourcing, and we do not all have to be Jack of all trades.

In addition, investing does not always mean that you have to get the highest returns in the market. Some people are just okay with average returns, so long as their investment keeps growing. You would rather grow your wealth slowly, while you concentrate on other equally valuable things like your job and your family, as another takes care of your investment because it is his area of specialty.

Index Funds Allow You to Retain More of Your Money

Jack Bogle occasionally warns investors not to allow the tyranny of increasing costs to overtake the magic of multiplying returns. This means that if an actively-managed fund beats an index fund such as the S & P 500, it really shouldn't matter even if that attracts huge fees, even if it's up to 25% of the investment.

Luckily, this is not how index funds operate. First, they have the advantage of only attracting minimal fees, and the investor gets to keep more of his money, both the principal amount and the returns. The low fees are courtesy of low operating costs, little or no commissions charged and tax efficiency.

Liquidity

Index funds are liquid. In this case, liquidity refers to the flexibility of buying or selling index funds as the trading day closes using the value listed as of the fund's net assets. Although the liquidity of index funds is not like that of stocks, which can be sold and bought at any time in a trading day, they are still some of the liquid options available. ETFs can fall in any of the two classifications because besides offering diversity, they are managed just like stocks and can be traded quite easily. Their prices are also updated throughout the trading day just like those of stocks. Every time you buy or sell them, you will use real-time prices.

Diversification

Index funds track indexes that contain a large number of securities therein. By itself, an index is already diverse because it takes in securities of different firms. It is also possible to enhance this diversification by adding more index funds of a different kind, and they will also be carrying multiple securities. The advantage is that this level of diversification reduces the risks investors open themselves up to when they hold individual stock and other investments that deal with narrow market segments.

Tax Efficient

When using a taxable account to invest, instead of IRA or 401(k), opting for index funds will help you not just minimize the costs of operation, they will help you reduce the taxes you owe. Typically, investors owning mutual funds have to pay taxes for their share of the capital gains each year. Since active funds have to be traded on a daily basis, a large fraction of the gains from them is taken as short-term capital gains that are taxed using the income tax rate. This is different from long-term gains derived from investing in index funds, which attract a 20% tax only. Therefore, holders of actively traded funds end up paying higher taxes than those who have invested in index funds.

Low Risk but Grows Steadily

One of the primary advantages of index funds is they are a relatively low-risk option for investing in the stock and bonds market, which makes them steady and suitable for long-term investment. The funds are diverse and will represent different areas of the economy in only one index, which is good because one stock preserves the other by absorbing the losses. Overall, index funds perform better in the market than many different kinds of investment vehicles that strive to beat the market on a daily basis.

Fees Are Low

Investors in index funds part with far much less in costs compared to those investing in actively-managed funds. Even when the actively-managed fund performs better than the index fund, it must do so by such a large extent to ensure that the returns it generates are high enough to absorb the high fees charged for it to be said to be doing well in the market. One of the reasons the fees inflate is the constant transactions that must be done to ensure that the investment competes in the market. This is unlike index funds that stick to a particular index and are traded passively and so, and its fees are much lower.

Provide for Efficient Building Blocks

Index funds are excellent building blocks for a broader range of financial assets not only because they are less demanding but also because of the diversity they introduce, which will make your investment portfolio as a whole diverse. They are also low cost and offer good returns in the long-term, which provide the money required for other investments.

Perform Competitively

Although index funds are not out there challenging other stocks through regular trading, they are competing in silence. Index funds aim to offer the investors returns over time, and most certainly, as you have already seen, their yields are much higher than that of other investments in the long-term.

Transparent

In their approach to investment, index funds are open and straightforward. They seek to produce good results in alignment with their market benchmark, the index. This method of having an underlying benchmark increases the transparency because the performance of the index itself is open for the public to see.

A Low Turnover

Index funds have a lower turnover than their counterparts, the actively-managed funds. The turnover ratio of a mutual fund is the amount of the fund's portfolio that has to be replaced annually. For example, if a mutual fund has made an initial investment in 100 stocks and 50 stocks are replaced in only one year, then the fund's turnover ratio is 50%. High turnover increases management and maintenance costs. It is also likely to attract additional taxation through capital gain distributions.

No Manager Risks

The manager risk is the risk that a portfolio manager will make grand mistakes that will cost you the performance of the stock. This commonly happens when dealing with actively-managed funds. The issue here is that it is impossible for a fund manager to avoid making mistakes, despite his experience, skill and education level. A human is prone to making errors, and managers are likely to make mistakes centered around timing or selection of the wrong securities. These mistakes are primarily driven by emotions like fear, greed, or a miscalculation of the investor's sentiments.

However, since index funds are managed passively and automatically, these mistakes are a rare occurrence.

Takes Out Psychological Pressure

Index funds would be a suitable option for people that innately have problems with math. This is by no means insignificant because it can have an incredible effect on a family and its finances. A miscalculation that leads to investing in the wrong stocks could lead a family to financial ruin. It is also a fact that many people in the society do not have a basic grasp of the interaction of numbers.

Take the example of the following question about a bat and a ball:

The total cost for purchasing a ball and a bat is $1.10. However, the price of the ball is $1.00 higher than that of the bat. What is the cost of the ball?

Many people give $.10 as the answer, and they are wrong. The price of the ball is $.05. This demonstrates how difficult it either can be for some people to grasp a hold of the numbers because they lack the interest or do not understand diversification math. They do not realize that on an average, and individual stock can compound at a lower rate than a broad portfolio can, or that a number of bankruptcies for a number of holdings can still produce positive returns.

The index fund resolves these issues by burying all individual returns of the component stocks, so the investors do not have to think of them, and this encourages them to hold on longer than they would have had they dealt with the falls and rises of individual stocks.

Diffuses Possible Biases

Index funds distribute the risk of various biases such as irrational escalation suitable for persons who are not adept in business matters. Many people lack an understanding and even fear the financial markets. This is the case for many beginners especially; they only hear of terms used in these markets but do not understand what they mean. Concerning choosing stocks, a majority of them is not able to value businesses and otherwise, would be ruled out in matters business. It is not uncommon to find people who outshine the rest in other areas of life make poor investment decisions by dumping all their savings in companies and stocks they do not understand, with ridiculous reasons to back their poor option. However, an index fund helps to eliminate this risk, especially when backed with professional advice from a mutual fund company and from individual financial experts.

Makes the Portfolio More Comfortable to Manage

Investors do not have to wonder about the small details of their investments or about how individual stocks are performing. All that they have to do is to ensure that they balance out the portfolio and keep rebalancing it occasionally.

Index Funds Automatically Cleanup

The manner in which index funds are created allows an automatic cleanup of the portfolio. Stocks that outperform are retained while underperformers are taken out. This keeps happening now and then based on a critical evaluation of the market. Therefore, when an investor decides to purchase index funds, he does not have to worry that laggards will take up his investment.

Index Funds Can Adapt to Efficient Markets

Across the globe, investors have been observing that as the markets become increasingly efficient, the managers of these funds are frequently having problems with beating the benchmarks. In a market like this, passive funds are the preferred vehicle for investment. It has been observed that in the segments of the market that are most efficient, passive funds are significantly present.

Minimal Maintenance

Many people are looking to save and invest in ventures that will not cost them their sleep. They want to "set and forget" once they have done their part. Those investing for their retirement, in particular, hope to have comfort in their old age after retirement, and not hovering around trying to maintain and secure their investment. Index funds allow investors to sit back, relax and focus on other areas of life.

Average Returns Are a Guarantee

Most people seeking to invest always aim to have performances that are higher than the average, but the majority of them do not achieve this. In fact, a significant proportion does not even get to average returns. However, this is guaranteed in index funds investment. The fund itself is the average. Therefore, once you have made your initial investment, be happy to know that you have already achieved average returns.

Index Funds Outperform the Majority of the Actively-Managed Funds

If you still do not find the assurance of average returns reassuring enough, then think about this: what if you invested in actively-managed funds and there is a pretty good chance, about 80%, that you will end up with less money? Actively-managed funds seek the services of investment experts and analysts who are intent on achieving huge returns but they rarely, if ever, reach the success an index fund does. On the other hand, when you choose index funds as the investment vehicle, there is a 4 in 5 chance that the returns you get will be better than those you could have obtained had you invested elsewhere.

Gets You on the Same Boat with Others

When you own an index fund, you have simply combined stocks that could be bought individually into one bunch. Therefore, when other stockholders do well, you know that you are doing well too, and if their stock is performing poorly, so is yours. Thus, when the market has gone down, and the investment suffers some losses here or there, take comfort in the fact that you did not cause the failure by when you picked the index you chose. On the other hand, when the market is up, also relax, knowing that you too are prospering just as the rest of the market does that too.

Beat the Financial Managers

Research has shown those fund managers who are entrusted with the responsibility of picking the stock rarely beat the indexes. Therefore, when you buy your stocks in an index fund, you are likely to see better returns than the active fund managers do because their focus is to determine the next big win and not overall profitability.

Chapter 8: Possible Downsides

In this new age, index funds are becoming increasingly popular, primarily because of the modern portfolio theory which claims that markets are increasingly becoming efficient and that the price of a security is now determined by all the information about it that is available. As a result, actively managing a fund today is now pointless, and the investors would now be better off purchasing index funds and going their way instead of constantly monitoring them.

However, from observation over many years, you can indeed conclude that the prices of stocks are not always rational. This factor alone profoundly opposes the idea of efficient markets that control themselves. Therefore, although many financial experts are now professing that investing in index funds is the way to go, many reasons besides the unpredictability of markets that oppose this. These reasons include:

Index Funds Lack Flexibility

Since persons managing index funds must follow particular rules and employ specific strategies that require them to follow in the footsteps of the index, the managers do not enjoy the flexibility that other managed funds provide. Index fund investment decisions must be made in the presence of all the constraints that the matching index will present. For example, if the returns on an index are declining dramatically, a manager is limited in what he can do to avert the losses. This is unlike the manager of an active fund because he has the opportunity of finding options that perform better, whether the market is doing well or dismally.

The Gains Are Not Big

An index fund is not able to overtake the market as managed funds do. Therefore, when you decide to invest in index funds, you are forfeiting the possibility of acquiring massive gains. In a given year, the top-performing non-index funds have better returns than the top-performing index funds. The only problem is that the best performing non-index funds do not stay at the top all the time, their performance varies from one year to the next, which means that the top performers will be canceled out if the funds underperform in the next year. However, index funds are steady in their performance.

The Passivity of Index Funds

By design, index funds are purely passive. They move in step with the movements of the market and try to invest across a wide array, as much as possible to avoid large value plummets. On the surface, this is a genius idea because this makes index funds quite safe. However, in the event the market itself is flooded with unsafe stocks or has stocks whose value is inflated, then when the inevitable crash happens, it will destroy the value of the index fund.

An actively-managed fund is unlikely to suffer a fall as huge as that of an index fund because the managers can monitor the market and identify all the unsafe funds and avoid trading in them. If the risky stocks are already in the investor's possession, then he will implement the "buy low, sell high" rule to avoid losses.

A good example is the Nasdaq index fund that was selling quite fast during the 1997 to 2000 dot-com bubble because it focused its attention on technological developments that were beginning to surface. Although the index itself fell in value after a short time, individual investors got the opportunity to avoid the losses. Some were quick to sell it early or hung on to companies that survived the decline such as Amazon whose share price fell from $107 to $7. Although, companies like it rebounded radically in the decade that followed.

A Lack of Control

The fact that an investor will be involved in support of all manner of companies included in a particular index is a disadvantage. This is because if an investor does not like a company on personal or moral grounds, yet the company is one of those included in an index he has purchased, the investor does not get to remove his money from that company without forfeiting the investment he has made from other companies listed in the index fund. When dealing with an actively-managed fund, however, it only takes a call to the manager, and you can have your money withdrawn from that company.

A Balance of Risk vs Rewards

Investing is usually compared to gambling, the legal form of it, at least. However, instead of putting your money on balls bouncing on a wheel, an investor places his money on companies he bets will do well in the future and avoids those he suspects will not do so well. However, when it comes to index funds, this form of "gambling" is similar to betting on red in each game. Yes, this is safe, but this safety is both an advantage and a disadvantage. Choosing the investment you want to make and then leaving your money with a trader is even riskier because it introduces human error. However, it is also in this submission that the benefits arise, and this makes the difference between index funds and managed funds.

Index Funds Lack Downside Protection

The stock market has proven itself as a viable investment ground over time despite running into some bumps on the way. For example, when you invest in an index fund tracking the S & P 500, you will get the notion that the upside of the market is doing well. However, there is nothing to shield you from the downside, and you will be left completely vulnerable. You may wisely choose to hedge against this exposure by shorting the index or purchasing a put against that index, but since these moves will be moving in entirely different directions, using them defeats the entire reason for your investment.

Underperformance

Since your index fund demands that you pay management fees, expect to perform slightly worse than the index will do. A portion of your returns will be subtracted to cover these fees, or you could be asked to dig into your pocket and pay upfront, depending on company policy. This slight performance is a disadvantage but is allowed because there is no way that you could afford to purchase stocks from each of the companies listed in your index. The conveniences of owning a variety of stock at one buy make up for the slight lag in performance.

Index Funds Are Non-reactive

It is not unusual to find some mispriced securities in the market. For example, if a company is getting a unique benefit, in sympathy, all other like companies will have the value of their stock shifted upwards. This leads to overvaluing the entire group. The reverse can also happen where a company that is performing dismally takes down with it the prices of the stock of other like companies.

Active management of stocks may take advantage of this change in the market. For example, an investor could take note of all undervalued stock identifying them by various factors other than price and purchase them while overvalued stock can be sold at a profit.

Indexes do not allow this kind of advantageous behavior. If a stock is overvalued, it is allocated even more weight in the index. Unfortunately, this should be when the investors note this and act by lowering the contact their portfolio has with the overvalued stock. Therefore, even when an investor has caught wind of the overvaluing or undervaluing of a particular stock, having invested in an index fund, he cannot act upon this information.

Limits the Investor's Exposure to Diverse Strategies

The world of finance has numerous strategies that investors take up in the pursuit of success. Unfortunately, once you have invested in index funds, you are not able to use up many of these good strategies and ideas. For example, some investors combine investment strategies and come up with returns for which the risk has been adjusted better. Although index funds provide you with one of the most useful tools, diversification, it only allows you to invest in as few as 30 stocks and not the entire 500 stocks that the S & P 500 Index tracks.

In active management, however, an investor can continuously monitor the market and conduct research that will enable him to identify the best growth stocks, the highest value stock, and other stock that rank highest in various categories. The investor is also able to implement different business strategies which when combined produce the best, more targeted and well-positioned investment portfolio that brings in good returns. In addition, the new portfolio will be more adaptable to risks and more suited to your likes, preferences, and tolerances.

Reduces Personal Satisfaction

The entire investment process can be stressful and unnerving especially when the market is changing drastically. Choosing some stocks may lead you to always glance at the market quotes and unable to sleep. However, these problems do not go away when you simply want to invest in an index, and you could still find yourself becoming apprehensive, wondering how the stocks are currently performing in the market. With this kind of worry, it is likely that you will lose all the enthusiasm, excitement and satisfaction that comes with making a good investment and achieving financial success. You are unlikely to make similar investments in the future.

Index Funds Are a Boring Investment

The idea of financial "gambling" is that it should produce new highs and lows through some losses and some incredible gains. This is the thrill of broking and other similar activities. However, if you yearn for this kind of excitement, possibility, and risk, opt for alternatives like individual stocks, hedging or additional high-risk actively-managed mutual funds. Index funds are naturally boring because an investor only has to place his money in an index fund and sit back, waiting. Although this is unexciting, a large percentage of investors, at least 95%, will tell you that this is the best strategy.

Diversification as a Disadvantage

Diversification in the index fund investment sphere can also be a disadvantage. Say, for example, that you bought Apple shares in 1990 while the prices were still low, you would have made a lot of money from them now. However, had you invested in an index that contained Apple stock in 1996, it is likely that you would still have the money you initially invested in, although you would have made quite some good returns. However, these returns would not be as much as those you would get from investing in Apple shares alone.

Come to think of some of the legendary investors, for example, the Oracle of Omaha himself, Mr. Buffet, it is possible that he would not have achieved the level of business success he has now had he diversified and bought 1,000 stocks. It is likely that we would not even know he existed. Surely, he would have made some considerable amount of money but not enough for the world to consider him the investment guru we now call him.

Buffet made a lot of money because he exerted much of his effort, attention, and finances on his most promising ideas. Buying an index fund spreads your interest in a number of companies, and this kind of divided attention does not result in much success.

Therefore, although diversification is functional because it insulates you from having to experience losses when certain shares in your index fall, there is a whole load of companies that are doing well, and you could reap mega-profits if you picked several company's stocks and invested heavily in it. Using Buffet as an example again, reports say that he owns stock from about 50 companies now which is a small number considering the amount of wealth he has and the fact that he has assembled an investment team to scout the market and determine the best investments to make. Had his diversification been too good, he would have bought stock from so many companies.

Index Funds Returns Are Considered in Hindsight

When discussing the profits of an index fund, financial experts and investors consider the returns the index has been producing in the past. However, the decision of whether to invest or not should not be determined by past success, but by future projections, because the risks that could shake up the performance of the underlying index are either in the present or in the future, and not in the past.

If indeed you decided to factor in the risks that have shaken up the performance of the index in the past, or even project future threats, that would still not provide an accurate evaluation because we are living in a volatile world. There is no telling the developments that will come up in the future courtesy of rapid technological advancement and the effect that these changes would have on the market. Financial experts foresee the growth of an efficient market, but as we have seen, there cannot be a perfectly efficient system because different things are continually coming up shaking up the foundation of the financial market. Therefore, if a company's stock has a history of performing well, you never know what would come up and suddenly, the company as a whole would be considered redundant.

The disadvantage of investing in index funds because of these factors is that some companies are likely to shelter behind the efforts and success of others comfortably, and when their stocks fall, the loss will be spread across the companies in an index. However, an individual who has purchased shares is less likely to feel the effects of shakeups like those because most companies tend to take up measures to ensure that they shelter against risks and shakeups, to avoid being written off. Therefore, while holding stocks, it is likely that you will continue to enjoy returns whatever changes come, and whichever the market situation.

The Disadvantage of Comparison

When scouting the market searching for the right index, potential investors tend to take up a lot of time comparing the performance of one index fund against that of another. For example, they may check to see the star ratings of each fund. When you do this, and some actively-managed funds perform better than the index you purchased, you are likely to feel bad and to regret your decision. Whether it is rational or not, this disreputable behavior of comparison derails index fund investments.

There Are No Big Winners

If scoring big in the financial market excites you, then index funds are not for you. This is because even in the event of a big win on one stock, the money will be spread across the shares in the index. Therefore, even when individual company stock is doing so well in the market, you are unlikely to see a spike in the value of your index fund. Therefore, before you own an index fund, ensure that you can take its slow yet steady pace.

Overall, an investor should examine the disadvantages listed above before deciding to invest in index funds. Once you are comfortable that you can handle them all or can find ways to shelter yourself from a number of them, nothing should stop you from moving along and investing in these true profit-makers.

Chapter 9: The Future of Index Funds

The beauty of index funds investing is one secret that the world is now awakening to. Many people are now focusing on this investment vehicle, with a number of investors shifting billions of dollars in investment from actively-managed funds to the passive index funds. This increased popularity is worrying some, based on what happens with many good investment ideas; they crushed once the secret was out. Is this what is about to happen to index funds?

Size challenges the outperformance of any investment, but this may not be the case for index funds. Primarily, index funds are weighted by the market capitalization of their companies, and flows that go into index funds that have been weighted in this manner ought not to influence the stock market because stocks are bought according to the size of the current market cap. This is to mean that by purchasing, you will not be overweighting or underweighting any securities. In fact, buying and selling forces should not impact the index funds market because they are essentially the market.

In a way, anyone worried about the increased popularity of index funds is wondering how the equity risk premium occurs in the first place. They are wondering, now that everyone knows that index funds offer a substantial long-term bonus, why wouldn't this risk premium go away eventually?

The answer is that the funds would be preserved because investment is behavioral. First, it is assumed that investors are loss averse which means that instinctively, they are more sensitive to losses than to gains. Secondly, it is expected that even the long-term investors who invest based on the "set it and leave it" investment behavior, they still evaluate their investments frequently.

For index funds to become too popular such that their viability as excellent investment vehicles is challenged, the investors would have to be behaving perfectly. Besides, for every winner, which the stock market is mostly about, there is always someone in the middle and a loser at the back. Some people will purchase the poorly performing indexes and opt out while others will remain at the top. However, it is unlikely for an index fund to be at the top all the time, you can expect ups and downs with each. This means that there will always be a rhythm, which is the thrill of risk and investing. It is likely that index funds will maintain the top quartile of all long-term funds regarding performance unless actively-managed funds dramatically lower their fees.

You can also rest assured that asset allocation will remain a primary determinant of the performance of your portfolio. Underweighting or overweighting particular market segments will always make the performance of your index different from the total market index or the S & P 500, and this variance is what determines your returns and your risk profile. Because of this, it is likely that the investor flows will impact asset classes, but it is expected that they will affect the performance of a market capitalization weighted index.

Do not even worry about what would happen if everyone on the planet or at least, 80% of us invested in index funds because that would not occur in the first place. Human nature would not allow it.

Today, indexing only accounts for 5% of the total trading volume in the market, which is indicative that actively-managed investments will always have a larger share. It is, however, likely that the returns from the stock market will get lower with time, but that will not be because the index fund market is getting crowded.

Conclusion

Thanks for making it through to the end of *How to Start Your First Index Funds Investment: A Beginner's Guide to Low-Risk Investment with Index Funds*. Let's hope it was informative and able to provide you with all of the tools you need to achieve your goals whatever they may be. You are certainly impressed by the amount of information you were able to take in and how much more confidence you have in your ability to plunge into the world of investment and succeed at it!

Index funds are a compelling investment vehicle. The long-term funds offer you a whole lot of benefits such as low taxation, lesser risks, and the assurance that your money will keep growing over time. You do not have to keep checking on your money to see how it is doing or even worry that the stocks therein are performing poorly in the market. All you have to do is sit back and wait for your index funds to mature before you redeem the money at a predetermined time. There isn't undoubtedly a more natural way to make a passive income.

The next step after learning about this incredible investment is to put this rich knowledge into practice. You have seen the need for urgency because the sooner you invest, the sooner your money will begin to grow and multiply. In this market, you are likely to find a good index fund that will not hurt your pocket. Go on, take care, and avoid miscalculations if handling the investment process by yourself, and if using a fund manager, which is preferred, choose a reliable one with good credit. Look around the market and conduct research until you are confident that the index fund you select is ideal. When you do this well, you can immediately join the bandwagon of investors singing praises of index funds because as you have seen, with this investment, returns are guaranteed.

Finally, if you found this book useful in any way, a review on Amazon is always appreciated!

28465211R00076

Printed in Great Britain
by Amazon